All Things Are Possible

(Page 3)

To Include:

All Things Exist

(Page 13)

All That Is Divine

(Page 19)

All That You Behold

(Page 29)

Neville Goddard

All Things Are Possible

n the ninth chapter of the Book of Mark, it is said: "*All things are possible to him who believes*," and in the nineteenth chapter of the Book of Matthew we are told: "*With God all things are possible*." Here we see God equated with the believer.

Seated here tonight you believe you are a man or a woman. You believe you are here, but are you willing to believe you can go beyond what your reason and senses dictate? You do not have to limit your power of belief to what your reasonable mind dictates. The choice and its limitations are entirely up to you, for all things exist in the human imagination and it is from your imagination that your belief stems. If you go beyond the dictates of reason, it must be via your imagination, and since all things now exist there, you can at any moment go beyond what your reason and senses dictate.

We have just had an eruption in the Christian world concerning the little icons people have made and worshiped for over a thousand years. The 115th Psalm described them as: "*Their idols are silver and gold, the work of men's hands. They have eyes but do not see; mouths that do not speak; ears that do not hear; hands that do not feel; feet that do not walk and no sound is heard in their throats. Those who make them are like them; so are all who trust in them*."

In today's paper the story is told of a famous actress who had an accident while in her Rolls Royce. She was injured, but not seriously and attributed her luck to the little icon she called St. Christopher. She is just like the one who made it and sold it to her, but she doesn't know it. Don't judge another by their worldly possessions. They received them through belief, but they do not know their very being is the one who created it for them. She believed her little gold icon saved her from a fatal accident. Nothing saved her but her belief in it. She bought and believed in her little icon because she does not know the one in whom she should trust.

All things are possible to him who believes and *"with God all things are possible."* Here we see that God and the believer are one. When you leave here tonight, you expect to find your home where you left it. You will go to sleep there and believe you will wake up in your bed tomorrow morning. You believe you are clothed right now. I tell you: your capacity to believe is the human imagination, which is the only God. All imagination, you have restricted yourself by the body of sense and reason you wear. Reason says you are in this room, that you have a certain amount of money and can have no more unless you make a physical effort to get it. But you would wish you had more wouldn't you?

Assume your wish through the sense of feeling. That assumption, subjectively appropriated and believed to be true, is faith. Can you believe in its reality? Knowing all things are possible to him who believes, can you persuade yourself that, although your reason and senses deny it, your assumption will make it so? Blake, in his wonderful "Marriage of Heaven and Hell," said: *"I dined with Isaiah and Ezekiel and asked: Does a strong persuasion that a thing is so, make it so? and Isaiah replied: All prophets believe it does, and in ages of imagination a firm persuasion moved mountains, but many today are not capable of a firm persuasion of anything."* Everything here was once only a desire, believed. This building, the clothes you wear or the car you drive were first a desire, then believed into being.

Yes, I believe there is a man named Neville. He may work for you to aid the fulfillment of your desire, if you believe you have it. Many men can and will come to aid you, even without knowing they are doing it, if you believe. You do not have to persuade others to help you; all you need do is believe you are what you want to be and then let the world (which is nothing more than yourself pushed out) go to work to make your assumption possible. I promise you: your desire will be fulfilled, for all things are possible to him who believes.

The late Robert Frost said: *"Our founding fathers did not believe in the future, they believed the future in."* The most creative power in you is your power to believe a thing in. Our founding fathers did not believe that the passage of time would produce this country as they desired it. They wanted democracy, not a monarchy, and knew that sitting down and hoping it would come to pass wouldn't do it – they had to appropriate it, so they simply believed it in. How? By faith. They subjectively appropriated their desire.

Let us say you would like to be in San Francisco now, but you don't have the time or the money to make the trip. What do you do? You ignore the present moment and subjectively appropriate your objective hope by sleeping in San Francisco tonight. As you lie on your bed, look at your world through the eyes of one who is sleeping in San Francisco. You may wake in the morning to find you are still physically in Los Angeles, but while you slept changes were taking place which will compel you to make the journey. I tell you: you will always go physically to the subjective state you have appropriated.

Remember: all things are possible to him who believes, and with God all things are possible. Man believes that God created the world and all within it, but he does not equate God with himself, the believer. But the Bible equates God, the creator of everything, with one who believes. And belief need not be restricted, but can go beyond the evidence of sense and reason.

In the world you must go on the outside to light your way. You may light a candle, a lamp, or use electricity; but one day you will turn within to discover that you are the light of the world. Then you will know you are God, the light of infinite love, infinite power, and infinite wisdom. You will expand into these states as you break the barriers of reason and senses. I challenge you to examine yourself. Are you holding to the state you desire to experience? Test yourself, and as you do you are testing Christ, for he is God's power and wisdom. It doesn't cost anything to test him, so try it.

We are told that imagination speaks to us through the medium of dreams and reveals himself in vision. One night I was shown how to test myself. That night I found myself in an enormous mansion on 5th Avenue in New York City at the turn of the century. Everything that money could buy was in that mansion. Although I was invisible to the two generations who were present, I could hear everything they said. The older gentleman spoke, saying: "Father used to say, while standing on an empty lot, 'I remember when this was just as empty lot,' then he would describe the building he wanted to be there as though it were already solid and real." Then the scene shifted and I saw the building, now complete, standing where only a moment before had been an empty lot. The grandfather was now standing next to his son and grandson and said: "I remember when this was an empty lot."

This dream taught me a marvelous lesson. I was the grandfather, the son, and the grandson. It was up to me now to pass this knowledge on to other generations. While standing in a barren state you can say: "I remember when this was barren." If it was barren, you are implying it is no longer so. Then you can – by exercising your inner sense of sight, sound, taste, smell, and touch – occupy the state and allow it to externalize itself for you. I tell you, it does not matter what you have or who you are in this world, all things are possible to you when you believe.

You may believe in one or more of the ninety odd so-called saints which have now been demoted, but if you believe, they have served their purpose. Now those who formerly believed in icons on the outside must turn around and learn to believe in themselves. It has taken a long time, for more than a thousand years men have believed this nonsense. You don't have to cover your head any more to enter the church – so was it ever necessary? You don't have to believe in St. Christopher any more. It never was necessary; but man, in his child-like state, could not believe in himself, so he created something with his human hands to believe in and his belief produced itself. The icon did not do it for the individual. His belief did it for him.

All things are possible to him who believes and with God all things are possible, so is God not one with the believer? His name forever and forever is I am. Do you not know that you are? Knowing that, are you not saying: "I am"? If your name is John, you must be aware of it before you can say: "I am John." I say: "I am Neville." I may not always say "I am" before I say "Neville," but I am aware of being Neville before I say the word. I have given my awareness of being a name. It is Neville. I do not have to repeat the words "I am" to define what I am aware of; but my awareness is God, the believer, and there is no other God.

Now, all things exist in the human imagination – not just the good things, but all things. Listen to these words from the 32nd chapter of the Book of Deuteronomy: *"See, I, even I am he and there is no God besides me. I kill and I make alive, I wound and I heal and no one can deliver out of my hand."* Who can kill but God? You may say: "I killed him," but that is God's name. Your own wonderful human imagination has the power to kill and make alive, to wound and heal and there is none that can deliver out of your hand, for there is no god besides your own wonderful human imagination.

As you are seated here you have the capacity to believe. You may believe in something stupid, but you believe and your belief will make it work. The one I speak of as God is your mightier self, yet your slave, for purposes of his own. He waits on you as indifferently and as swiftly when your will is evil as when it is good. He does it by conjuring images of good and evil just as though they were real. Allowing you to imagine whatever you desire, he projects it upon this screen of space in order for you to experience it. You can move into it so naturally and so easily you can forget the thoughtless moment when the seed was planted, and therefore do not recognize your own harvest.

The being you really are is the God in scripture who is your own wonderful human imagination. Can you leave this auditorium tonight in the deep conviction that you are what you want to be? Are you willing to assume its joys and woes? Your assumption is your subjective appropriation of an objective fact. That is faith and without faith it is impossible to please him.

Tonight, when I leave this building I will ride home with my friend. As we travel we will pass certain streets and see familiar objects because we will be traveling by sight. But when I walk by faith my steps are invisible, for I will be walking in the assumption of my fulfilled desire. Paul tells us to *"walk by faith and no longer by sight."* We all know what it is like to walk by sight, but now we are called upon to break that spell and walk by faith.

I tell you it is possible to be anything you want to be, for the believer and the God of the universe are one. Don't divorce yourself from God, for he is your I Amness. Believe in your I Amness, for if you do not you will never fulfill your desire. Only by assuming you already are the one you would like to be will you achieve it. It's just as simple as that.

I am not saying it's easy, but it becomes easier with practice. If I gave a Stradivarius to one who had mastered the violin he could lift me to the nth degree of joy, but if I put the same violin in the hands of one who could not play it, he would shortly drive me insane. It's the same violin, yet one brings harmony while the other brings discord. You kill and make alive out of the same instrument, which is your own wonderful human imagination. You may make many discords until you learn how to play. We are here in this world of educated darkness learning to play the instrument which is God. You may not know anyone who would give you $10,000 right now, but if you believe all things are possible to God and you know that God is your human imagination, you can imagine you have the money, persist in your belief and you will have it. How, I do not know; I only know that according to your belief will it be done unto you.

Do you believe that all things are possible to God? And do you believe that he is your own wonderful human imagination? Knowing that God is all love, and you are capable of imagining unlovely things, you may not believe your imagination is God, but if that is true then God is not all-powerful. If you can imagine something that God cannot, then you transcend him. If God strikes only harmonious notes and you can strike chords that produce discord as well as harmony, then you are greater than he because you can do something he can't. But I tell you: your own wonderful human imagination kills and makes alive, it wounds and heals, for all things come out of the human imagination. While learning to use and believe in your human imagination you may make alive that which you do not want. You may wound yourself in the process, but what you create in your imagination you can uncreate.

Everything can be resolved, even though while learning, horrible mistakes are made. Don't condemn yourself for anything you have ever done, are doing, or may do, as you learn to play the instrument who is

God himself and your own wonderful human imagination, for there is no other creative power.

What is now proved was once only imagined. My tailor uses his imagination to execute my suits for me. They must first be imagined before the cloth is cut. My tailor doesn't take his scissors and start cutting the cloth in the hope that something will come out; he imagines it first. And when I sit in my barber's chair he sees what ought to be on my head instead of what is there. Everything must first be imagined before it can become a fact, and that capacity to imagine is God.

Now, you do not observe imagining as you do objects in space, because you are the reality that is called imagination. You can observe this room, which was once only imagined, but you cannot observe the creative power that conceived it. The things created are seen, but you – the creator – are not seen, and you will never know you are He, until God's only son, David, stands before you and calls you Father. Not everyone will accept this knowledge, for they would rather have their little icons. I'm quite sure this Italian actress who had the accident would not be interested in or believe my words, and she is not alone. There are hundreds of millions tonight who would not give up their little medals. I saw where Cardinal McIntyre had put his seal of approval on the reverse side of the little St. Christopher medal, thereby giving it his blessing. On one side is a face that never existed and on the other, a priest of the church gives his approval. What nonsense, yet the medals work because people believe they do.

It's time for man to stop believing in something on the outside and start believing in his human imagination. It's time to stop all the outside icons. *"You shall make no graven image unto me, or have no other gods besides me."* You may have no education, no money or social background, and find it difficult to believe in yourself; but because all things are possible to him who believes, and with God all things are possible, you can go outside of your senses and believe anything into being. Test your imagination, and if it proves itself in performance, what does it matter what the world thinks?

Through testing I have proved imagination. I have found him and now I share my findings with another. He is called Philip, the lover of horses, the symbol of the mind. Knowing Philip loves learning about how the mind functions, I tell him that "I have found him whom Moses and the law and the prophets spoke – Jesus, the Messiah. I will take you to him." You are here because, as Philip, you desire to know more about the mind and its functions. I can take you to Jesus by telling you who he is, but I cannot show him to you, for he is invisible.

Your I AMness is he. Say: "*I am secure, I am wealthy, I am free.*" This may not be true based upon your senses, but I am simply asking you to say the words, for the moment you do you are subjectively appropriating security, wealth, and freedom. Reason will try to take these from you, so I ask you to play a little game with me. Go through the door and walk as though you are secure, wealthy, and free. Sleep this night as though it were true. If you do, you will not fall asleep seeing the world as you did last night, you will see it differently. If this morning someone gave you a check for $20,000 and you deposited it to your account, you would be $20,000 richer, therefore you could not sleep tonight as you did before. Now, without waiting for someone to physically give you the money, go to bed as though it were true. Put Christ to the extreme test. If all things are possible to God and if all things are possible to the believer, can you believe? I am not saying you will succeed the first night, or even the second. Having been trained to accept only what your reason and senses dictate, you may find it difficult, almost impossible, to believe what you could believe – but you can!

This morning as I was returning to this world I came upon a scene of shadows of beings. The first one was blind, unable to see the world round about him. The second one saw, but his vision was limited. The third saw more than the second, and the fourth could see, hear, and do more than the third. I awoke, saying to my friend Bob Crutcher: "With your talent to write, you could write a movie about this series of events. If you did, you would receive $3,000 for it."

I knew that just like an actor I had identified myself with every shadowy being I had seen. Although shadows, I, the perceiving one, had assumed one after the other to find myself limited by the state perceived. As I assumed the first one I was totally blind. As the second I could see a little, and as the third a little more. Then I woke urging Bob to write it, to show how man is restricted by what he is wearing.

In order to play a part, you must feel the part. As the blind man I had to feel my way about. When I put on another garment I could see and did not need to feel any more. With each garment I wore, I sensed more and more, and awoke urging my friend to show this in picture form in the hope that those who would see it would understand that man is only playing a part. The part need not be that which was given him at birth. He could pick a part and enter it at any point in time.

Right now, you are playing a part. If you don't like it you can change it. You could play the part of a man wealthier than you were twenty-four hours ago. It's only a part for you to play, if you desire it.

Everything I am telling you is from the Bible. "*I kill and I make alive. I wound and I heal and there is none that can deliver out of my hand. I, even I am he and there is no God besides me. I am the Lord your God, the holy one of Israel, your Savior and besides me there is no savior.*" These are the words of God, revealed through his prophets of old. Their prophecy is fulfilled in the New Testament as: "*Whatsoever you desire, believe you have received it and you will.*" That's how easily you apply it, for an assumption, though false and denied by your senses, if persisted in will harden into fact.

I am telling you: you are God and there never was another. The being in you is God, and you and I are one, because there is only one God. In the end you will know that you and I are one, for you will discover you are the father of my son, who you will know to be your son. In fact, it will not be the son revealing you as the Father, but you, the Father, revealing your son.

Now let us go into the silence.

All Things Exist

"All that you behold, though it appears without, it is within, in your imagination of which this world of mortality is but a shadow."

William Blake

he world of imagination is infinite and eternal, whereas the world of generation is finite and temporary. In that eternal world, the permanent realities of everything exist. Their reflections are here, cast in a glass called nature.

> *"The oak is cut down by the a*
> *And the lamb falls by the knife,*
> *But their eternal forms exist forever,*
> *And are renewed by the seed of contemplative thought."*
> *(William Blake)*

The permanent realities of an extinct bird, animal, or fish, live! They can be resurrected and externalized by the seed of your contemplative thought, for everything lives within you!

This world of generation I call the world of Caesar should not be neglected, as it is an important aspect of reality, even though it is only a shadow. Scripture urges us to revise, to forgive, and change our thoughts, thereby changing the conditions of our life. This is how it is done.

A friend recently wrote saying: "Three weeks ago a friend called, saying he was afraid he was going to be fired. I instantly revised his call. Hearing his voice bubbling with excitement, he told me how he had been praised for his work and I felt the thrill of rejoicing with him. Today he came to my office and said the very words I heard in my imagination.

"This morning, while dressing I was thinking about an ad I was working on which carried the name of a very prominent man in San Francisco. As I ran the ad through my mind I said to myself, I want to put the word 'Mister' before his name. I did it and it felt right. I made a mental note to do it when I arrived at the office, and promptly dropped the thought. That afternoon the man called, asking that I insert 'Mister' before his name – not in the ad, but in a radio commercial where his name was used."

Then my friend added this thought: "I stand in awe at the operation of this law. You asked about the little pig I saw. He was small, but fat, and the way I am stuffing him today, in no time at all he will be so large he will fill this room.

For those who are not familiar with this symbol, the pig is the symbol of Christ, the power and wisdom of God. Every time you exercise your imagination lovingly on behalf of another or yourself, you are feeding Jesus Christ. My friend is stuffing his pig, because every moment of time he is alert and putting this law into practice.

Now a lady wrote, saying: "I found myself looking at an enormous building at the edge of a vast body of water where your classes were held. A man at my side asked: 'How do the students get to the classes?' Pointing to another student who was walking on the water towards her destination I answered: 'That's how it is done.'" "Unwilling to accept my answer the man said: 'But how do you do it?' and I confessed: 'I have placed stones just below the water.' Then the scene changed and I am with a friend who said: 'I am pregnant.' Shocked, because I knew she had no husband I asked: 'By whom?' and before she could answer, I awoke.

"Three nights later I found myself in a very large building containing a theater, where you were the one actor who was playing every part. As you assumed the role of the blind man, I realized there was no one to lead you, so I ran to help. As we walked, we came upon a young boy sound asleep. Then you said: 'I told him to meditate and he has fallen asleep again.'

"The scene changed, and I am viewing paper decorations hanging above a door. I reached up to pull them down, when an enormous wind caught me and I felt as though I was borne in the arms of a very strong man and awoke saying, '*I love thee, O Lord.*'"

This marvelous series of dreams revealed much. This lady admitted crossing the water while walking on a solid foundation. Now the Bible is a parable from beginning to end, and water is the symbol of its psychological truth. The literal interpretation of a parable is solid as a rock. When the meaning behind the parable is discovered, the stone is rolled away and the water found. However, if a little solid reality in this world is desired while playing with this psychological truth, it becomes stepping-stones below the water. Loving what is heard is not enough. One must be willing to go all out and walk on the water. Instead, feeling she must be practical as she was living in a world of reality where rent must be paid, food bought, and clothes purchased, she is unable to walk by faith at the present time.

Let me give you a definition that came to me concerning the word faith. Faith is the subjective appropriation of an objective hope. When my friend revised the first telephone conversation, he subjectively appropriated what he hoped would objectify for his friend. He remained faithful to his imaginal act, and confirmation came.

Do as my friend does, and you will experience the glorious sensation of walking on the water in your mystical world. In my own case I was pulled by a wonderful goose, the symbol of the Holy Spirit. Having lassoed him with a silver chain – the symbol of knowledge – he propelled me over this fabulous water. This is He who will lead you into all things, as recorded in the 14th chapter of the Book of John.

The lady saw the protean man when she saw me playing all the parts. As the dreamer of the dream, she has been impregnated by the one she spoke to when she awoke, saying: "*I love thee, O Lord.*" Mary did not know the name of the one who impregnated her, yet it was the same Lord, the same I AM.

In this lady's dream she was so brutally honest with herself when the man insisted that she tell him how she crossed the water. She could have said she walked on the water. Instead she told him exactly how it was done, thereby admitting to herself that she has not gone all out and lived by the law, but has a little anchor on the side, in the event it doesn't work.

In Barbados we have a saying: "I have a hind-claw," meaning there is some money tucked away in the bank, a little income from the family, or something I can fall back on just in case. We have these beach crabs on the island that are almost impossible to catch. Running at top speed, the crab can run right over a precipice and disappear. If you followed him you would break your neck in the fall, but the crab has a hind-claw that stops his fall. He grabs the earth just below the surface, and there the crab can pause and get his breath before climbing back and entering the race again. I urge you not to have a hind-claw. Be for me or against me, but be one way or the other.

Now, I want to share an experience of a lady who wrote, saying: "About a year ago I was deeply concerned for my mother. While lying on my bed, I began to imagine her face radiantly happy, and hear her tell me she had never known such happiness before. As I listened, I heard my name whispered softly three times.

"Startled, I raised myself off the pillow to see you standing in mid-air. Dressed in a gray suit, you smiled, raised your arms, and removed the eyes from your head. Then you came over and calling me brother, you pressed them into my eyes. Bending your head, I watched it grow transparent and enormous in size. Then I saw that every living thing in the universe was there. You straightened up, and as you did your head returned to its normal size. Again, raising your right hand, you took off the top of your head and handed it to me, where I saw the greenest of green grass growing there, and you vanished."

Yes, I called this lady brother advisedly, for regardless of the sex worn here, we are immortal brothers, all of us. So, I say: "Go unto my brothers and say to them, '*I have ascended unto my God and your God, unto my Father and your Father.*

It was over a year ago when I placed my eyes into her sockets and gave her sight. Now she has become the incurrent eyewitness. In her vision she saw a long table. A man dressed in the white robe of a judge, carrying a gavel in his hand, entered the room. Looking directly at her, the gavel hit the table and he said: "I pronounce you the incurrent eyewitness."

The word incurrent means, giving passage to a current that flows inward. This lady is now so conditioned that I can reveal all things to her so that she can know the truth of the statement: "All that you behold, though it appears without it is within, in your Imagination, of which this world of mortality is but a shadow." She saw that every living thing was contained in my immortal head. Destroy the garment I now wear or anything in my world and I will reproduce it again, for my immortal head cannot be destroyed.

Start now to practice what the Bible calls repentance, which is a radical change of attitude. No matter what it is, if it does not conform to your ideal change it by subjectively appropriating your goal. Remain faithful to it and no earthly power can keep you from attaining it.

Go all out and walk on the water! Don't be like Peter, whose understanding told him imagination didn't make sense (symbolized as his feet), or you will drown in the sea of illusion. Imagination, speaking to his faith, said: "Peter, come," and as Peter walked, he looked down to see how this was possible, and sank. My friend, who did not look down, walked on the water in the direction of his wish fulfilled – and it was.

All of the Bible stories will be fulfilled literally on different levels of your being. You will experience them all, because you are Jesus Christ. Blake tells us so beautifully: *"Desires and perceptions of Man, untaught by anything but organs of sense must be limited to objects of sense; therefore, God becomes Man that Man may become God."*

If you only knew what your organs of sense reveal, you would never perceive anything beyond them. It would be horrible to remain an organ of sense and never transcend it. But God brought creation with him when he became humanity, and you are here to awaken to that fact! If God did not become you, you would be an animated body, limited to all that your sense organs would reveal. But having become you, God is awakening and will give you desires and their fulfillments, far beyond the wildest dreams of those who are still limited to the organs of sense.

When Blake said, *"All that you behold, though it appears without, it is within you,"* he meant it. Being an incurrent eyewitness like my friend, Blake saw God's mystery of salvation clearly.

I urge you to exercise your divine right by using your imagination. Be like my friend who is now consciously feeding his pig. Every moment of time you have the opportunity to feed your pig. When someone phones to tell of their misfortune, revise their words. Go about your business of creation on the inside, and do not do a thing on the outside. Use your imagination and let your words come into being!

All things are possible to you, because you are all imagination and imagination creates reality. Knowing what you want, imagine you have it. Knowing what you want to be, imagine you are it. Subjectively appropriate your objective hope and you have assumed a virtue you did not have. Ask no one to help, and do not feel below the water for something to fall back on if imagination doesn't work. Instead, learn to count on your true Self, who is Jesus Christ!

Jesus, your own wonderful human imagination, is your hope of glory, and there is no other Christ. Defined as God's power and wisdom, Imagination is in travail until Christ is formed in you. On that day your history will be changed from BC to AD, and every year thereafter will be the year of the Lord. Having been formed in you, Christ is born, and the words of Isaiah become yours: *"For to you a child is born and a son is given. The government shall then be upon your shoulders, and you will be the Wonderful Counselor, Mighty God, Everlasting Father, Prince of Peace. And of your reign there shall be no end."*

Start now to look upon the great mystery of creation as the subjective appropriation of your objective hope. Dwell upon my words. Put them into practice, and you will experience their fulfillment, for all things exist within you!

Now let us go into the silence.

All That Is Divine

n the nature of things, it is impossible for any child born of woman to go unredeemed, for the moment he says, "I am," he is proclaiming all that is divine in his flesh. Therefore, God cannot cast away that which constitutes the "I" of man without casting himself away, and that is impossible.

Scripture teaches in the form of parables, and we must learn to distinguish between the parable told and its message. In the 18th chapter of the gospel of Matthew we read that he placed a child in the midst of them and said, "*See that you do not despise one of these little ones; for I tell you that in heaven their angels always behold the face of my Father who is in heaven.*" The word "angel" means "a messenger; to bring forth," and the word translated "child" means "an infant; a term of endearment." Here we find a child is always beholding the face of the Father who is in heaven and bringing forth his message by becoming what he beholds.

The reality of man is symbolized as that of the Christ-child, the incorruptible seed which is always beholding the face of the Father, molding man's reality into the Father's image that he may become one with his Father. Casting his shadow into a certain role, we judge the role, not knowing that the innocent child is doing it as he molds himself into the image of the Father. In the world we play our parts by saying, I am rich, I am poor, I am known, I am unknown; yet all the while the innocent Christ-child (this incorruptible seed) is beholding the face of the perfect one, molding itself into the image of that which it beholds. It is my desire to constantly see truth so clearly that I become its image and share it with everyone who will listen.

Not understanding the horrors of the world, man thinks he is damned and not saved; but I tell you, every child born of woman is already redeemed. The being that is the child's reality is molding himself into the image of the Father and becoming what he beholds. But in the world, he is casting himself into the many parts to be played. At the moment he may be playing the part of a rich man or perhaps a poor man; still he is free to choose yet another state by applying the precept, *"Whatever you desire, believe that you have it and you will."* You are always molding yourself into the image of what you are beholding, whether in this world of death or that world of life. But your Christ-child is always beholding the face of your Father and molding himself into his likeness, that you may know who you are and say within yourself, "I am He!"

This seems fantastic, but it is true, for I am telling you what I know, not what I am theorizing or speculating about. No one can fail. God hardened Pharaoh's heart so that he could not let his people go. Then giving them blow after blow, he again hardened his heart – so who is responsible? The child is dreaming he is Job as he casts his shadow and plays the many parts. But in the end, you will understand why you put yourself through hell, and you will be given a hundred times more than you had before.

You are playing a role now, and have played unnumbered roles in the past. Many of you here are playing the last role, but every role was for the purpose of molding you into the image of that which you are beholding. Always beholding the perfect image, hopeful that you will not deviate from it, you will become an image of truth.

Now he tells you, "If you abide in my Word you will know that I am the truth." You will know this when God's son sets you free, and when your son sets you free, you are free indeed. In the meantime, you are molding your face into the image of that which you are beholding. Now you see only the shadow world, but if you believe me and remember my words in your moments of despair, they will support you in your times of trouble.

In the eighth chapter of Proverbs, the little child tells us, *"In the beginning, when the Lord created the universe, I was beside him as a little child. I was daily his delight, rejoicing before him always. He who finds me, finds life. He who misses me, injures himself; all who hate me, love death,"* for they are in love with this world of death.

When you view consciousness you must see the two relationships: the pure, unconditioned I AM, and the conditioned I AM. Now conditioned,

I am aware of being Neville, a speaker and teacher. Another condition placed upon pure awareness is that of a banker, a lawyer, or that of a thief. These are all conditioned states of being the little child has cast you into, and you are playing your part perfectly.

You do not see that little child until the end of the play, at which time you will hold that infant in your arms and your intense feeling towards him will come forward into speech. In my own case I said, "How is my sweetheart?" The child calls forth a term of endearment, for when you find that child, you find life. You find he who was beside the Lord when he created the world, and you will know that. He who misses me, injures himself, and he who hates me is in love with the world of death.

Everything here is mortal, and in time the billionaire will leave his billions and the honored general will leave his medals. The billions will decay and the medals will tarnish. Everything here will vanish and leave not a trace behind, but he who played the part of the millionaire and the general cannot vanish. He is that little child within, who was one with God, and is God. It is he who watches and changes the image until he is as perfect as his father in heaven is perfect. He is building the same image and when he reflects and radiates it, you will find that child and speak words of endearment to him.

The child is but a sign of your true being who is casting himself into these many roles. He cast me into the role of a poor boy, in a family with no intellectual, social or financial background. Then he brought me out as the perfect image of the Father for me to discover my own being. That is the story of everyone in this world.

Now, he gives you a cushion by telling you that, through the act of assumption, you can fulfill every desire of your heart. Knowing what you want, you must assume that you have it in the same sense that the Christ child is assuming he is what he is beholding. You must behold yourself as secure if that is your desire. You must behold yourself as healthy if that is what you want. You must feel yourself into the state desired with the same persistence as Christ in you is feeling himself into the image of the Father, for he never deviates from that wish.

When you know who you are, you will discover that you are free to be anything, go anywhere and possess every desire of your heart. You will also know that, no matter what you have gone through, what you are going through or what you may go through, you will be redeemed, for he, in you, will not falter watching the face of the Father. As Blake said so beautifully, "You will see from what I teach, that I do not consider either the just or the wicked to be in a supreme state, but to be every one of them states of the sleep into which the soul may fall in its deadly dreams of good and evil when it left paradise following the serpent."

It was the serpent, the symbol of eternal life, that said, *"Did God say you would die? I tell you, you will not really die, but will be like God, knowing good and evil."* Eating of the tree of good and evil, you remain in the world as you judge another; but behind your mask is the Christ child, who is molding you into the image of the Father. If you find yourself in a state you do not like, apply this principle and assume you are free from all encroachments, knowing in the depth of your soul that you are seeing the face of your Father. When you first see him you do not know he is the Father. Just as a child knows its parents before he knows they are his parents, you will know God before you know he is the Father, and you know the Father before you know he is yourself. This is how consciousness awakens in the world.

The son of man comes to save those who are lost by their wandering consciousness. You simply wandered from the state, that is all. You are not lost. When you say, "I am" you are in, of and moving towards the I AM. Always in him and of him, you are moving towards consciously thinking from being the one I AM. Everyone is moving towards being that I AM, for everyone is in imagination, of imagination, and moving towards knowing consciously that he is all imagination.

Everything in this world invites you to wander away from the I AM. Urged to believe in that pill, this diet, a man, you move away from your true identity and become lost as your consciousness wanders. But it doesn't really matter, for you cannot be lost, as the son of man will come. He is the one in whom the ideal has been realized. Called Jesus, he is the personification of the incorruptible seed which awoke, budded, flowered, and bore its fruit. And in that state you move towards Fatherhood when your son David reveals your true identity.

Last lecture night I tried to make my message clear, but there were those who did not understand, so I shall repeat it briefly now. The message is simple. In scripture, the expression "Christ" is used of the human race and of the human who has achieved the ideal. The human race, with all of its generations and experiences, is personified as the eternal youth, David. Now the being in whom the ideal is realized, is called Jesus, who is God the Father, whose son is David. Everyone in whom the ideal is attained is Jesus, and in the end there is Jesus only, who is the one body, one Spirit, one Lord, one God, and Father of all. You, individually, will attain the ideal when you are confronted by your son who bears witness to the fact that you are God the Father.

This may not be the easiest thing to grasp, but you dwell upon it. Lean against this truth in time of trouble. That is what Paul meant when he said, "I consider the sufferings of this present time not worth comparing to the glory that is to be revealed in us." Paul never doubted this heavenly vision was the promise God made to the fathers, but he didn't spell it out. I am trying my best to make it as clear as possible. The sum total of your experiences in this world of humanity – no matter how cruel they may have been – when fulfilled, produce David; so in the end you will say, "*Father, forgive them, for they know not what they do.*" On this level we judge and condemn, but these parts must be played by you, an individual, before you can produce David, and when you see David you know you are God the Father and that is Jesus.

Now, he calls a child and puts him in the midst of them saying, "Let no one despise one of these, for I tell you that in heaven their angels always behold the face of my Father, who is in heaven." Why? Because a man always becomes what his "I" beholds. You can take anyone and represent him to yourself as the man (or woman) you would like him to be and, if you do not waver in that representation, he will conform to it. If you want someone to be big in your world, you must make him big in your mind first, and treat him that way morning, noon and night. If you see him as that being, he cannot fail, because he must become what you behold. But you cannot waver. The moment you listen to a rumor, you change the picture, and you cannot.

Many years ago, I read the story of famous theatrical mothers and their sons. One was Milton Beryl. He was her only child and she built her world around him. She would join the group of boys playing ball and tell them that Milton was the star, and whatever he said, they were to do. If they did not, she would take their ball and bat away. The story listed a dozen such children whose mothers held that ideal of their sons in their mind's eye. They did not falter and therefore their sons could not fail. They had to become what their mother beheld of them. If a mother compares her son to another child and finds hers wanting, she has broken the image. She sees him less than, but she must see him as great and never falter in her image of him if she really wants him to be great.

Now, there is something in you that has never taken his eyes off the face of the Father and will not deviate until you are perfect. In the meantime, it casts its shadow and you play the part of a bum, a part necessary to bring the image into focus. Then it will cast another image and yet another until you are perfect as your Father in heaven is perfect. But what is the reality of your flesh? "I am." When you say "I am" you are proclaiming that which is divine and cannot be cast off unless God is willing to lose himself, for the "I" in you is God. Therefore, God cannot fail to achieve his predetermined goal, which is to fashion himself into and eventually become the Father.

What a mystery! Just think, before that the world was, you were predestined to become its author, its actor and the one who supports and sustains it. You, who have played many horrible parts, are Jesus. And when your image is perfect, you will awaken as he who is God, the Father of humanity. And when humanity is gathered together into a single being and projected, you will see your son David. That is the mystery.

What the next play will be I do not know. I only know that, until everyone has awakened, this play is not complete. So, don't criticize, or condemn, because – from above – we will aid every being here to come home. We are the ones called, *"Those who came to save the lost."* First we seek him, then save him by bringing that wandering consciousness back to the vision of the Father. Now my one consuming desire is to see truth so clearly that I become an eye-witness and can tell my experiences just as they happen m me.

I am not asking you to stop giving your money to charity if – in the giving – it gives you pleasure; but giving to the poor and needy is not going to save you. Only that which is in you, whose face is focused on the eternal Father, can save you by becoming what he is beholding. As he sees it, he casts its shadow. Knowing you need a certain experience embodied, he casts its shadow, yet gives you a cushion, telling you that whatever you desire, if you will but believe you have received it, you will. You may now be cast in the role of a poor man, but you need not anchor yourself there by claiming you cannot become rich. Rather, you can cast yourself in the role of a rich man by believing you are rich. You can cast yourself, consciously, into any role you desire to express while you are molding yourself into the image of the Father.

The Bible is filled with wonderful stories which the scholars have misunderstood. Like the one I quoted today. "He put the little child in the midst of them." Scholars wonder who the little child was and what became of him, for they read it as a secular story and the Bible hasn't a thing to do with any happening on earth. Jesus is not a man of secular history. He is a representative of every man within whom that incorruptible seed blossomed and bore its fruit. The resurrection, the birth, the discovery of the Fatherhood – all of these are the fruit you are bearing.

There is nothing comparable to this truth. If you owned the world, what would it matter if tomorrow you died and left it all? What would be the point of living if there were no end to this mortal life? But what I am telling you is true. You are an immortal being who cannot die. Dead though the body seems, you, its reality, cannot die for your I AM is God. There never was another God and there never will be another God.

You are slowly awakening to the realization that you are the God who created everything and that no one is greater than the other. In this world we all try to be better than the other, but when the truth is revealed, we will know that there is only one son and only one Father. And, if I am the father of David, and you are the father of David, are we not one? Then we will understand the great Sh'mah: "Hear, 0 Israel, the Lord, our God, the Lord is one." He is the one Father, and cannot be two, but if he is a father there must be a son to bear witness to his fatherhood. If you have the identical experience as I do are we not one? So in the end there is only one God, one Father, and one son. The one fell asleep and is dreaming this scattered, divine state into being. In the end we all will awake as the one who fell asleep, yet we will not lose our identity. I will love you dearly as a seeming other, yet know that we are one. It's a peculiar mystery. We are all God the Father, for there is no other being. God first reveals himself as almighty power, then as "I am" and finally as infinite love, the Father.

So, why are we here? Blake put it beautifully: "*We are put on earth a little space that we may learn to bear the beams of love.*" In your present state you could not stand the beams of love, for God's infinite love is sheer power. We see power used in going to the moon, and we contemplate going to Venus and Mars, but the power to get us there is as a firecracker compared to your true being who brought the world into being and sustains it.

One day the play will be over and, I don't care what a man has ever done, he will awaken as God. Put yourself now, in the part of a father whose son is accused of a horrible act. Loving your son, would you not want him to go free? I know I would. I would regret that he did it, but I would forgive him and want him to go free. Read David's story carefully and you will find that there is not a thing that man could do that David did not do. He sent Urias into battle, knowing he would be killed so David could have Bathsheba. Although he had a thousand wives of his own, he stole a man's wife because he wanted one more; yet he was called the perfect man, the Lord's son, "*A man after my own heart who will do all my will.*"

David is not a little man born of a woman. He is spirit. Personified as an eternal youth, David is the result of your journey into the world of death. When the Christ child, in you, has put you through all the generations of men and you have experienced everything you agreed to in the beginning, you are perfect as your Father in heaven is perfect, and you have formed David, your son, to reveal you to yourself. The world thinks Jesus Christ is the son of God, but I tell you Jesus is the Lord. This is a mystery. David comes in the spirit and calls Jesus "Father." Humanity is Christ, the son and Jesus is God the Father.

I cannot open your skull and force the solution to this mystery into it. I can only give it to you in words, but I can tell you that the day is coming when you will experience my words. Your skull will explode and you will experience everything said of Jesus Christ in the first person, singular, present tense. Cast in the major role, you will know you are he, even though you will remain a very limited being in this world of mortality. You came into this world of death to overcome it, bringing with you the incorruptible Christ seed who is beholding the Father, transforming you into his image. And since the Father cannot beget another, he is begetting himself.

But while you are here, take his wonderful precept and believe that you can have anything you desire. There is no restriction placed upon the power of belief. There is no need to first consult some holy man to see whether you should have it or not. You be the judge. Choose your desire and, to the degree that you are self-persuaded that you have it, you will get it. And, because we are all one, if it takes one million people to aid the birth of your assumption, they will do it, without their knowledge or consent, so you don't have to ask anyone to aid you. They will do it not even knowing that they are. All you are called upon to do is to assume that you have it. An assumption, though false, if persisted in will harden into fact. That is the principle.

Behind this fantastic play where you are awakening as God, we have a secondary state. In it you may be cast into the role of a poor man and need Caesar's coins to meet his demands of taxes, rent and food. So, you can render unto Caesar the things that are Caesar's by assuming that you have that which Caesar demands, and remain faithful to that assumption. In the meantime, something else is taking place in you which is infinitely greater than Caesar's world, for this world will come to an end, but the kingdom of heaven is forever as it is eternal. Caesar's world is one of death, but the human imagination is eternal life. It is the human imagination who will reveal your true identity to you when you are perfect as your Father in heaven is perfect. Then you will see David, the sign that you have reached the end of the journey. Having played all the parts, you are the conqueror and your crown is waiting for you as your son reveals your Fatherhood. If the Lord tells David, "*Thou art my son, today I have begotten thee*," and David calls you Father, are you not the one called God in scripture?

It seems so silly for a little man, one of billions, to make these extravagant claims, but they are true. Einstein was a man of small stature, but he conceived an idea that has changed the thinking of the entire world. So, God, wearing the mask of a little man, takes it off to reveal his true identity, and the little man's words, believed, will change the world.

So, the little child was brought and put in the midst of everyone. Don't despise him, for he is the one who was with me in the beginning of time. When I laid out the foundations of the world he was beside me as a little child. He was daily my delight, delighting forever in the affairs of men. He who finds him, finds life. He who misses him injures himself. He who hates him, loves death.

The little child is a symbol of you, molding yourself into the image of the Father. You are casting yourself into these shadow worlds and when you are perfect you will radiate your Father and bear the very stamp of his nature. Then David will stand before you, in the Spirit, and call you "Father."

Now let us go into the silence.

All That You Behold

*"All that you behold, though it appears without it is within,
of which this world of mortality is but a shadow."*

f you will but enter a state in your imagination, and assume its truth, the outer world will respond to your assumption, for it is your shadow, forever bearing witness to your inner imaginal activity.

Test yourself, and if you prove this to your own satisfaction you will come to the same conclusion the apostles did in the 13th chapter of the Book of Acts. Then you, too, will say: *"I have found in David, the son of Jesse, a man after my heart who will do all my will."* If the world responds to your imaginal activity, is the world not David doing your will? If the Lord claimed that David always does his will, and you, by a simple imaginal act, command the outer world to respond – are you not the Lord?

When you imagine something, it is as though you struck a chord, and everything in sympathy with that chord responds to bear witness to the activity in you. If the world is the responding chord to what you are imagining, and David is a man after your own heart who will do all your will – is David not the outer world? This is not "will" as the world uses the word. You do not will something to be so, but imagine it and become inwardly convinced that it is so. And if, through your persistence, the world responds, you have not only found David, you have found the Lord as your own wonderful human imagination.

In Hebrew thought, history consists of all the generations of men and their experiences fused into one grand whole. This concentrated time, into which all the generations are fused and from which they spring, is called "eternity." In Ecclesiastes we are told that "God put eternity into the mind of man but so that man cannot find out what God has done from the beginning to the end." Only in the end will you really know what God has put into your mind.

The Hebrew word, "olam," (o-LAWM') translated "eternity" or "the world" in Ecclesiastes, is quite often translated as "a youth; stripling; young man." These are three titles given David, the son of Jesse. And the word "Jesse" means "any form of the verb" to be", *i.e.:* I AM." Is that not God's name? When the time of your departure has come, you will see the world of humanity, not as a crowd of people, but as a single youth, a stripling, a young man; for eternity is personified as the youth called David. You will know this to be true only when you reach the end.

Now listen to these words found in the twentieth chapter of John: *"Peter went into the tomb, where he saw the linen clothes lying and the napkin which was on his head lying – not with the linen clothes – but rolled up in a place by itself."* You may wonder why this is stated thus, but I tell you: the linen clothes and the napkin are very significant. Read the story carefully and you will discover the tomb where he was crucified and buried was called "the skull". And Peter, when entering the tomb, saw the linen clothes and the napkin, but could not see the one who was put there.

This is not a secular story of a man who died wearing linen clothes with a napkin covering his face, and left the tomb three days later, leaving his clothes and napkin behind. No, scripture is vision filled with symbolism. The linen clothes symbolize your physical body, the garment you wear here which covers your true identity. This is not a story of one who has died, but of one who has risen from the dead!

In ancient times, the word "napkin" had a far wider range of meaning than it has today. We have a dinner napkin, a cocktail napkin, and also a sanitary napkin; but this napkin symbolizes the placenta, the afterbirth. The napkin appears, separate from the body, to tell you that a birth took place. This is the birth John insists is necessary for entrance into the kingdom of heaven.

Matthew and Luke tell the story of the birth as a woman called Mary giving birth to a little child who was different, yet born as we were born. But when you read the story in John (the most profound of all the New

Testament writers) you discover where the birth takes place, and who Mary really is. Mary is the skull, the womb God entered. Blake said: *"God Himself entered death's door with those who enter. And he layed down in the grave with them in visions of eternity until they awake and see Jesus and the linen clothes lying there which the female had woven for them."* My mother wove this fleshly garment that I wear, and when I came forth it was from her womb; then the placenta followed. It had to be discharged, for it has no part of the earth. So, it is with the napkin, telling you here that an unusual birth has taken place in the skull, where the drama began and ends!

No doubt unnumbered millions attended last Sunday's services and heard that he has risen. Yes, he has risen, and so will you; for God actually became as you are, that you may rise to know yourself to be as He is. Having entered your skull, he now has visions of eternity. Visions of wars, famines, and convulsions, were first imagined, or they could not happen. When you imagine a state, and find its response coming from without, you have discovered who God is, for all things are made by him. As he wills it so, so it is; but he must have one who will do all of his will.

If it takes five hundred different beings, male and female, to respond to your imaginal act, they will come and seem to you to be the influence through which your desire is made visible. You see, humanity is David, always doing your will; and when your time is fulfilled, the whole of humanity is fused into a single youth and personified as David. Strangely enough, he comes from within you and reveals you as his Father. Then, speaking from experience, you will say: "I have found David. He has cried unto me, 'Thou art my Father.' "and you will know your journey is at its end. It takes all the generations of men and their experiences to bring you to the point of confronting the beauty of those experiences, fused into a single youth known as David.

Every child born of woman will eventually know that he is the God who created the universe and willed everything into being. Then he will forgive all, for he will know they were only doing his will. Then everyone summed up will appear to him as David, and he will say, "I have found my son David to be a man after my heart who does all my will."

Now we come to these words: "*I, Jesus, am the root and the offspring of David.*" Yes, the day will come when you will know you created, entered, and animated humanity, so that they could respond to your imaginal acts. And when you have played all the generations of men and had all of their experiences, you will come out of humanity knowing you are its offspring and its root, therefore its Father; yet you come forth from the Father as you promised yourself you would.

You are told: "When your days are fulfilled and you lie down with your fathers, I will raise up your son after you, who will come forth from your body. I will be his father and he shall be my son." Having created humanity, awareness came forth and buried itself in humanity; for a seed must fall into the ground and die before it is made alive. Unless it dies, it remains alone; but if it dies it brings forth much. God died to become humanity, which is made of the dust of the earth. His name is I AM. That is the seed which fell into the earth called Man (humanity); and every Man (be he male or female) says "I AM." If I AM is imagining a certain state and the world responds (be it good, bad or indifferent) is the response not doing my will?

Whether the response comes from a single person or unnumbered people, they are David, for it is he who is always doing the will of I AM. Regardless of your present name, color, or race, you are David when you respond and make visible to me that which I have imagined. And when you find the cause of the response, you find it in yourself.

Test yourself, and you will discover that your imaginal act was the cause of the response of the world relative to you. Then you will have found the Father and the son and your journey will be at its end, for you will have set yourself free from secondary causes in this world of death. Then your journey will fuse itself into a single youth called David. You will recognize him as he is, just as described in the Book of Samuel. You will see eternity, which God buried in your mind; and you will be enhanced by reason of the experience of creating these bodies for the stage, entering them, and playing their various parts.

Your presence here tells me you have played them all, because no one comes unto me save my Father calls them, and I and my Father are one.

Your consistent attendance and your interest in my words tell me you are at the end of the play. Having played the part of the well-known and the unknown, the wealthy and the poor, the disgraced and the proud, you have played everything, as it is all contained within you. Every conceivable part is now a reality in you, but you need not activate it. You can, however, enter a state and by the simple act of assumption, activate that state, and not one power in the world can stop its response. If it takes a dozen or thousands of men and women to respond to your assumption, they will, for humanity is David – a man after your heart who will do all your will.

Everyone necessary to fulfill your assumption must and will come to bear witness to that which you are entertaining, internally. Now, although Nicodemus was a member of the Sanhedrin and knew Hebrew thought concerning history, he could not comprehend the idea of a second birth. It was he who asked: *"How can a man who is old enter his mother's womb a second time and be born again?"* Then the answer came: *"You, a master of Israel, yet you do not know; except you are born from above you cannot enter the kingdom of heaven called the new age."*

This is a drama of one being, expanding himself by first creating humanity, and then limiting himself to his creation. Humanity, although part of the structure of the universe, is dead. God, breathing upon it, possesses the body and Spirit, enters, and animates it. Now, in a body that is dead, God will go through the horrors of the journey, dreaming you and your experiences into being until he awakes where he began the dream – in Golgotha, his tomb, which is your skull. And when God awakes, you awake. As you emerge from it, you will look back to see that which you occupied for six thousand years. You will see the linen clothes which your mother wove in her womb, and you will leave the napkin which the body expels.

Then those who come to bear witness to your birth will see only the discarded body and that which symbolizes your birth from above. Having had the experience, I can tell you: you started your drama in the skull and you will end it there. The drama is all about God, for he created it all. It is God who is playing all the parts of the drama and in the end, it is God who extracts himself and rises from his own dead state. That is the resurrection. If you think in terms of one little being called Jesus Christ, you miss the truth completely; for Jesus Christ is your own wonderful human imagination who is God himself. When you imagine a state, God has imagined it; and just as a sound brings a response, your world will respond by playing the part it must play to bring about fulfillment.

All you are required to do is remain faithful to the state you entered. Now, Paul makes this statement: *"Remember Jesus Christ descended from David according to my gospel."* Having experienced scripture, Paul calls it "my gospel." He does not deny the descent of Christ, yet he knows that David was created by him. Having buried himself in David, God died by forgetting himself. Then David appears as memory returns, and he extracts himself from that body to discover he is far more luminous than he was before he entered it; far more translucent, greater in power and wisdom than he formerly was; for God is truth and truth is an ever-expanding illumination.

There is no limit to expansion and luminosity. There is only a limit to contraction and opacity. Resurrection is simply rising from the body of death in which you are now encased, and expansion is yours because of your willingness to come into this world of death and overcome it. So don't look for any little napkin on the outside, for it is only a symbol of your spiritual birth. When the vision comes upon you, you will know what has happened and why John placed such importance to the napkin. It was John who emphasized birth from above, for only after that kind of birth can Fatherhood be discovered.

Afterbirth belongs to the body, but after the offspring comes out, the afterbirth is discharged. It is a sign of birth which can be seen; but no one can see you with the mortal eye, for yours is a spiritual birth. They will come and see the remnant you wore, but you they will not see. The day will come when you will experience the symbolism of scripture. Then you and I will once more be in that one body we occupied prior to our descent into these bodies of death. The body of the Risen Christ is not something that is finished, but is in the process of erection. Made up of the redeemed, everyone must rise to that experience, thereby making the body more glorious, more luminous, and far more wonderful, than it was prior to our descent into our own creation of death.

You did nothing wrong which caused you to enter a body of death called Man. You were in the beginning with God and were God. You never were some little worm, which – coming out of the slime – became a little bird and then something else, to evolve into man. No, all this is part of the structure of the universe. You were God when you descended into and animated man; and no one can descend into humanity other than a son of God (of which there is a definite number) and it takes all of his sons to form God.

The word "God" is plural. The word is "*elohim*," which is a compound unity of one made up of others. It takes all of the sons of God to make up the I AM; therefore, there can't be more in this world then there are God's sons. Every child born of woman is alive because a son of God (his ancestral being) is in him, animating him and putting him through the paces until he detaches himself from that body which is his David, his beloved, just as the world is.

Someone sitting in a dungeon feeling abused can enter into an image of hate and cause disturbances in the world. Although he is completely unknown and buried in a dungeon, thereby unseen by the world, he can imagine with such intensity that many will be caught in its response. We are forever giving advice, when scripture has nothing to say about advice – be it good or bad. Scripture only tells us to go and tell them the good news that you are immortal, as they are. That you created the world and simply extracted yourself from it, just as they can. Don't give them any advice as to what they should or should not do.

If your son wants to grow a beard, let him. If he doesn't want to grow up, don't try to give him all of your "good" advice; simply leave him alone, and in your own wonderful way imagine you are free of that state, for the world belongs to you and it is always expressing your inner thoughts. See a situation as something on the outside, and you become entangled in its shadows – for everyone who responds to your imaginal act is a shadow. How can a shadow be causative in your world? The moment you give another the power of causation, you have transferred to him the power that rightfully belongs to you. Others are only shadows, bearing witness to the activities taking place in you. The world is a mirror, forever reflecting what you are doing within yourself. If you know this, you are set free and a series of events will unfold within you to reveal the story of salvation.

Then you are urged to tell your brothers, to encourage them, for everyone is your brother. Go and say to your brothers, "I am ascending unto my Father and your Father, unto my God and your God." In the end we are one wonderful being. The body is now being slowly erected out of the redeemed, and everyone will be redeemed. If a brother is lost in the world of death, I will leave the ninety and nine to go in search for him. Everyone must be redeemed or the temple would be missing a stone; therefore everyone – even the Hitlers, the Stalins, all the so-called monsters of the world – will be redeemed, for they only respond to the fears and horrible thoughts men set in motion.

A friend wrote, saying that although she rarely buys a paper, she bought a Sunday paper a few weeks ago. In it she read a story of a woman who called herself a great medium. Believing that California was going to drop into the Pacific Ocean, she and her family were moving to Spokane. A few weeks later a friend came to call and brought a current paper. Glancing through it she found a story about the same woman who – although only 29 years old – upon arriving in Spokane she had a heart attack and died. All right. As far as the lady is concerned California did vanish. She is now in a world just like this, in a section of time best suited for the work yet to be done in her to bring her to the knowledge of who she really is.

This frightened little thing died so very young, yet while she was here she frightened so many in this state. Friends of my nephew moved to Arizona, not realizing that they were taking their beliefs and fears with them. You can go from here to the ends of the earth. You can make your bed in heaven or in hell; but you will still be aware because God is there, for you can't get away from being God. You may not know that you are, but if you are afraid here you will be afraid there. Like Job, this lady's fears came upon her. Being afraid, she created her own disaster. But at the end of Job we are told that it was God who wrought it, for only at the end of the journey do we realize who God really is.

Having heard of him with the hearing of the ear, when our eyes behold the truth from experience, we understand. Afraid, I prayed to an external God, and all of my fears came upon me. Then, seeing the symbol that reveals my Fatherhood, I said: "I have heard of thee with the hearing of the ear, but now my eye beholds thee." When God extracts himself from this fabulous experience, everything that he was is doubled. That is the story of Job. He did nothing that was wrong; Job simply imagined the wrong things. He blamed the devil, but the devil doesn't exist outside of man.

Satan is the doubter. It is he who doubts the reality of your imaginal acts. If you can't believe in the reality of your unseen imaginal act, you may turn to another and believe in him; but you are always imagining, for imagination is God, and imagination – imagining – is the power of the world. In the beginning you heard, but as your eyes see the result of your inner hearing you believe, and in the end, everything taken from you will return one hundred-fold.

Yesterday the world celebrated the resurrection, yet resurrection and birth from above are two sides of the same coin and take place the same night. The priesthoods of the world marked the time as the first Sunday after the full moon in Aries, but it does not have to be then. Resurrection can take place at any moment in time. It has taken place and is still taking place; for the temple is being rebuilt on a more glorious scale, for we are the living stones, forming the new Jerusalem. Believe me when I tell you that your own wonderful human imagination is Jesus Christ.

Imagination entered death's door (your skull) and is dreaming the world in which you live. It is imagination who will emerge, and when he does, you are Jesus Christ. There never was another Christ and there is only one. When I awake, I am he. When you awake, you are he. And when all awake, we are all he, who together form the one Lord God and creator of it all. Don't envy anyone or condemn anyone, for condemnation is judgment and judgment is a sympathy of your imagination. With what judgment you judge, you will be judged and fulfill!

You will always find people eager to question what you think of this one or that one. I am quite sure if we all traced our ancestry back far enough we would find hippies, murderers, and thieves recorded there. In the beginning no one was born a king; someone had to feel that position and take it by force. You don't have to go back and change anyone or anything, but envy no one. If someone wants a thousand or a hundred thousand acres, let him have them. If you would like to live in a lovely apartment, claim you do. You may think you can't afford the one you want, but that thought is an imaginal act. I would suggest, instead of thinking you can't afford it, to simply sleep in that apartment tonight mentally, accepting the fact that you have all the funds necessary to pay for it.

Persist and the world will respond. You will get the money needed to live there. The world does not cause, it only responds to your imaginal acts, for only God acts and God is in you as your own wonderful human imagination. Now, before you judge it, try it. If you do, you cannot fail, and when you prove imagination in the testing, share the good news with your brothers. Tell everyone you meet how the world works. You do not have to have a proper educational or social background to apply this principle; and you cannot fail, for an assumption, though false, if persisted in will harden into fact.

When you know what you want, assume you have it. Believe your assumption is true. Look at your world mentally and see your fulfilled desire. Do this and you are calling forth a response to your thoughts, and in the not distant future you will find yourself physically occupying the state imagined. Now, after you realize your desire, don't go back to sleep and hold on to this dream that is now solidly real, while trying to project a desire through secular means. We are warned against doing this in the parable of the rich fool, who said: "I have all that it takes, more than enough. I will pull down my barns and build bigger ones to store my grain and my goods. Then I will take my ease, eat, drink and be merry."

But the Lord said to him: "Fool! This night your soul is required of you." Don't hold onto anything on the outside; hold on only in your imagination. If something is taken from you, it is because at one time you assumed its loss and – for a moment – wondered what you would do if it were. You forgot the thought, but its message had already been released to fulfill itself. If you want to keep your possessions, you must hold onto them in your imagination and not build barns to house them.

Don't forget (remember) the story of the birth as told in John. He does not describe it as Matthew or Luke do, but tells you this birth is essential in order to enter the new age. Then at the very end he gives you this beautiful symbolism of birth which comes through death, for it is only through death that one lives. A seed must fall into the ground and die before it is made alive. So, God dies, saying: "*Unless I die thou canst not live, but if I die I shall arise again and thou with me.*" And God rose!

Now let us go into the silence.

www.ingramcontent.com/pod-product-compliance
Lightning Source LLC
Chambersburg PA
CBHW020445030426
42337CB00014B/1412